D0370395

SHOOTING BACK

THE RIGHT AND DUTY OF SELF-DEFENSE

CHARL VAN WYK

WND Books

SHOOTING BACK
A WND Book
Published by World Ahead Publishing
2463 West 208th Street, Suite 201
Torrance, CA 90501

Copyright © 2006 by WND Books

All rights reserved. No part of this book may be reproduced in any form or by any
means, electronic, mechanical, photocopying, scanning, or otherwise, without
permission in writing from the publisher, except by a reviewer who may quote
brief passages in a review.

Cover Design by Linda Daly

WND Books are distributed to the trade by:

Midpoint Trade Books
27 West 20th Street, Suite 1102
New York, NY 10011

WND Books are available at special discounts for bulk purchases. World Ahead
Publishing also publishes books in electronic formats. For more information call
(310) 961-4170 or visit www.worldahead.com.

First Edition

ISBN 13-Digit: 9780979045110
ISBN 10-Digit: 0979045118
LCCN: 2006936588

Printed in the United States of America

CONTENTS

This book is dedicated to all the victims of crime—who did not have the means to defend themselves and to all those people living in gun-free zones—who do not have the right to defend themselves.

ACKNOWLEDGEMENTS

THIS BOOK has been a long time in the making. The original pressure to record my experiences after the St James Massacre came from my parents, Adriaan and Lauretta van Wyk. Thanks, Mom and Dad, for the encouragement.

Maureen Blackshaw has been a wonderful help in getting the project started. She typed pages and pages from my tape recordings of this story, as well as from our chats. Maureen, this book is finally published and is in part almost as much yours as mine.

I am indebted to Dr Peter Hammond, Director of United Christian Action, for introducing me to the Biblical worldview at a seminar in 1991. Thank you for being my mentor, friend and leader. I was made aware of my Christian responsibility to defend my country through his writing. His teaching on forgiveness has greatly impacted my life.

Larry Pratt's writing (in Chapter 9) made me aware of my Christian responsibility to defend my family and other victims from criminals. Thank you, Larry and Priscilla, for being so hospitable when I visited the U.S. Thank you, too, Larry, for giving up your precious time to support pro-firearm organisations by addressing politicians in South Africa. Had I never read your writings, I may not have been here to tell the story.

Maxine Case has been very patient with me through this project. Her inquiring mind has caused me to have to sharpen my

ACKNOWLEDGEMENTS

arguments to prove my case. Thank you for your professional advice and hard work in making the book look the way it does.

I am very grateful to Johan van der Merwe, Phyllis Laing, Jeanine McGill, Maureen Blackshaw and Rob and Christine McCafferty for proofreading this book and to Emma Potter and Fred Moore for helping with the computer work.

Sonja, my wonderful wife, thanks for your patience when I had to work on this project instead of spending time with the family. It is now complete.

My greatest gratitude is to Jesus Christ my Lord and Saviour, for His perfect way of salvation and the freedom He has granted to those who submit to His authority. His Law is perfect, converting the soul.

FOREWORD

SOME JURISDICTIONS in the USA have declared churches to be gun-free zones. As Van Wyk's experience illustrates, no place is totally safe—not even a church. The notion that declaring an area to be gun-free will keep criminals from maliciously using guns is ludicrous.

Any law that makes self-defence illegal or impractical is an illegitimate law, because such a law ultimately subjects people to the criminal element. When governments pass laws favouring criminals, then governments are on the wrong side and have lost their legitimacy.

If a people are willing to surrender to the government their responsibility to protect their most important right; their right to life, then there is no reason they will not surrender all the rest of their rights—to raise and educate their children, worship as they please, own property, engage in commerce and provide for their own health and welfare. And last but not least, they will have no way to insure the accountability of their rulers.

Gun control in the USA dates back to before the country achieved its independence from Britain. In early 1775, the British government ordered General Thomas Gage, the governor and military commander of Massachusetts, to capture a large cache of arms and gunpowder that were being stockpiled by the colonial militia. That effort culminated in ill-fated raids on Lexington and Concord, Massachusetts on April 19, 1775. These are regarded as the first battles of the American War of Independence.

In the early days of the American republic, gun control laws were passed to keep African slaves disarmed. Following the American Civil War, Jim Crow laws were passed for the purpose of keeping black persons in *de facto* servitude. Among those laws were restrictions designed to keep black persons (and only black persons) from purchasing and owning guns.

Restrictions on firearms ownership were enacted with general, non-discriminatory language throughout the USA during the last century. Initially, though, these laws were only applied to black people. One has to concede that there is less racial discrimination in the application of these laws in the twenty-first century. Now all people find it increasingly difficult to obtain and carry firearms. All people, that is, except the criminal element.

The British experience should dispel any illusion that it is possible to pass a law that will keep guns out of "the wrong hands." All legal handguns have been confiscated and the remaining old-fashioned rifles and shotguns must be kept under lock and key and unavailable for self-defence. Yet following the handgun confiscation in England, crimes committed with handguns jumped nearly 40% from 1999 to 2000. Violent crime in England now surpasses the U.S. violent crime rate.

In 2000, Georgetown University anti-gun scholar Jens Ludwig published a study in the stridently anti-gun *Journal of the American Medical Association*. He found that the Brady Law, which requires a background check designed to keep criminals from owning guns, has had no impact on lowering crime.

The American experience has been uniformly one of lower violent crime in those jurisdictions that make it legally easier for citizens to own and carry guns. The gun control Meccas of Washington, D.C.; Chicago, Illinois and Los Angeles, California are precisely the jurisdictions suffering high murder and violent crime rates.

It can be safely predicted that the implementation of the new gun control law in South Africa will have only one result—more crime, more people being murdered, more women being raped.

Those who support gun control support a very bloody law of unintended consequences.

I hope that Charl van Wyk's book will help turn the tide. South Africans—and people everywhere—need to refuse to support any laws that leave them defenceless against murderers, robbers, rapists and arsonists. If South Africans agree to live under pro-criminal gun control laws, they will have no right to complain when they and their families die or are bereaved at the hands of an unfettered and emboldened criminal element.

Larry Pratt
Executive Director, Gun Owners of America
August, 2001

INTRODUCTION

ON SUNDAY EVENING, 25 July 1993, I had just been singing with my daughter, Andrea, and was about to pray with her when the phone rang. It was my friend Marco:

"It was the worst nightmare, Peter; St James has been attacked by terrorists."

At the time our mission headquarters was in the same road as St James Church and several of our staff were members of the church. My father had been converted at St James.

As I sped to the church my mind reeled with the implications. I thought of my many friends there and prayed that they would be safe.

As if in sympathy with the storm in many hearts, lightning flashed across the sky and the heavens wept in a blinding downpour of torrential rain. Above the roar of the rain the air was filled with wailing sirens from convoys of ambulances, police vehicles and fire engines as they converged upon the scene. Flashing lights and flashing lightning illuminated a scene of dazed survivors fleeing from the church, weeping churchgoers praying in the rain and frantic relatives searching for loved ones.

I was soaked as I stumbled into the church. The tiles in the foyer were smeared with blood. There were several bodies lying on the bloodstained carpets or on shrapnel-scarred pews. Prayer books, music sheets, welcome cards and Bibles were strewn amongst the pools of blood. The ceiling was pockmarked with shrapnel.

Rescue workers were working swiftly and efficiently. Some of the wounded were being cared for inside the church. Others were being carried out on stretchers to the waiting ambulances. A broken pew was used to transport one person. Groups of Christians sat or stood holding hands and praying.

I located several friends and then began to help serve tea to the shocked survivors. Only later, as I began to hear the different testimonies of those involved, did the full scale and horror of the attack strike me. I also learned that after the grenades exploded, one of our members had returned fire with his revolver. The shooting stopped and the attackers withdrew. He then pursued the terrorists into the parking lot and fired at the getaway car as it sped away. When the police later recovered the terrorist's getaway car, the bloodstained seats indicated that at least one of the gunmen was wounded.

If one compares the St James Massacre with similar atrocities in Zimbabwe, Mozambique, Angola and Sudan—it becomes apparent that many more people would have died had Charl not fired back. His presence of mind, mental and practical preparedness and quick action had saved many lives.

When I saw the shocking carnage at St James Church, it immediately brought similar bloody scenes flooding back into my mind. Over the last 19 years of missionary work I have personally come across scores of similar atrocities, in Angola, Mozambique, Rwanda and Sudan.

In August 1983, Frelimo troops killed 5 pastors and burnt down all 5 churches in Maskito Village, Zambezia Province, Mozambique. In September 1983, Frelimo troops killed over 50 Christians and burned a church in Pasura village. At Chilleso Evangelical Church, in Angola, Cuban troops shot 150 Christians during a church service. At New Adams Farm in Zimbabwe, 16 missionaries and their children were murdered in November 1987.

Mobs have burnt down hundreds of churches and killed hundreds of Christians in Nigeria. In the Sudan hundreds of churches have been bombed and attacked by the National Islamic Front government. Many hundreds of churches were attacked in Ethiopia during the Marxist "red terror." And one could continue to recount literally hundreds of similar atrocities.

When the police arrested some members of the Pan African Congress (PAC) in connection with the St James Massacre, almost 1000 supporters of the PAC marched through Kenilworth and Claremont to demand the immediate release of their "freedom fighters."

I watched the mob dance and sing as they paraded past St James on Friday, 13 August 1993. They were on their way to the Claremont Police Station. The mob was chanting:

"Kill the Boer! Kill the farmer! One settler—one bullet! One minister—one bullet! One church—one bomb!"

The fact is that churches have often been the targets for terrorists.

On a recent visit to Zimbabwe, I took my family to visit the site of the old Elim Mission Station in the Vumba region. As so much of my mission work is spent helping persecuted Christians, I wanted to show my children an example of how Christians suffer persecution. I also thought that it might help explain why I must travel away from home so often to serve those suffering for their faith.

On 23 June 1978, terrorists who supported Robert Mugabe murdered nine British missionaries and four young children, including a three-week-old baby, at the Elim Mission Station. I showed my children the school buildings and we walked onto the field where the missionaries and their children had been herded, then tortured and bayoneted to death.

My point in explaining this atrocity was to illustrate the vicious hostility of communism to Christianity. However, the reaction of my children was quite different from what I had expected.

"Why didn't the daddies protect the mommies and the children?" asked my oldest daughter, Andrea.

"Well, these people were pacifists—they believed that they could never use any force to defend either themselves or their families," I answered.

"Then they couldn't have been Christians!" declared my younger daughter, Daniela.

"No, Daniela, actually these people were very sincere Christians," I explained. "They were very brave people who died courageously—even praying for the terrorists that they would be converted. They died as martyrs for Christ."

Andrea was horrified. "How could any Christian father stand by and refuse to defend his own children? The Bible commands fathers to protect their family!"

"You are right, Andrea. They were very wrong not to fight to protect their children, but they were sincere Christians all the same!"

"Well, I don't think they acted like Christians!" Daniela was adamant.

A long discussion over parental duties, self-defence, what constitutes a true Christian and all the related issues continued for days afterwards. Although Andrea was only eight years old at the time and Daniela was six, they were more concerned over the passivity of the parents than over the wickedness of the communists. Even our son, Christopher, who was only four years old at the time, was deeply offended and genuinely horrified that there was any father who would fail to do everything necessary to defend his wife and children.

"But if the bad people tried to hurt us you would shoot them, wouldn't you, Daddy?"

"Yes, Christopher," I assured him. "I most certainly would."

We discussed some of the Scriptures that clearly teach a man's responsibility to provide for the protection of his family: "If anyone does not provide for his relatives and especially for his immediate family, he has denied the faith and is worse than an unbeliever." 1 Timothy 5:8

Obviously I, as a husband and father, cannot only provide my wife and children with housing, food, clothing, education and medical care. I must also provide spiritual guidance, love and protection. "If a thief is caught breaking in and is struck so that he dies, the defender is not guilty of bloodshed." Exodus 22:2

"Like a muddied spring or a polluted well is a righteous man who gives way to the wicked." Proverbs 25:26

"Don't be afraid of them. Remember the Lord who is great and awesome, and fight for your brothers, your sons and your daughters, your wives and your homes." Nehemiah 4:14

From these and other Scriptures, it is clear that God holds men responsible for being armed and prepared to protect their families. In fact our Lord Jesus taught: "...if you don't have a sword, sell your cloak and buy one." Luke 22:36

Pacifist beliefs do not stand up to the harsh reality of our fallen world. Nor can pacifism be reconciled to the clear teachings of Scripture. "There is a way that seems right to a man, but in the end it leads to death" Proverbs 14:12

It is worth noting that the only British missionary at the Elim Mission Station who had a firearm—he owned a .38 revolver—was also the only survivor! Being cowards, the terrorists left him alone, preferring defenceless victims. The first the armed man knew about the attack was when he woke up the next morning to find the base deserted. He later discovered the bodies of his fellow missionaries on the sports field. Gun-free is no guarantee.

As Charl's story so clearly shows: armed citizens save lives, but unarmed citizens too often become helpless victims. This book is most important because it not only presents a seldom heard first hand perspective on a very key event, but it looks at the practical implications and what we can do to help save lives and prevent such atrocities recurring.

Dr. Peter Hammond
Director, Frontline Fellowship

PART ONE

CHAPTER ONE

ATTACK

*M*Y KNUCKLES WHITEN *as my fingers grip the cold steel. Motionless I stand at the entrance of the church. My eyes freeze, unfocused on the scene before me. It is like watching a replay of a sports match: you see it all and yet you see nothing. I am vaguely aware of the curdling screams coming from inside, but outside all is quiet, just that sickly sweet silence before we human beings are impelled into motion. Why am I standing here? Why do I have a revolver in my hand?*

To explain, let me start with what happened during the early evening of 25 July 1993.

It was a typical winter's evening in Cape Town, dark and dismal. The miserable weather mirrored the turmoil that the country was going through, while the people prepared themselves for the first general election in which all population groups could take part.

But back to 25 July 1993. It was my friend Keith's birthday and several of us had planned to meet at a steak-house after church to celebrate. Normally, our group would sit together in church, but somehow I sat alone that evening. Tonya, one of our friends, couldn't make it because her brother had arrived back home after many months at sea. Other friends had arrived late or did not see me as they entered the building. They sat elsewhere. The sanctuary was not as full as it usually was. There were slightly less than the approximately 1500 worshippers it normally held, which was probably due to the cold and rain.

The Reverend Ross Anderson opened the service after the choruses and first hymn had been sung. Two young members of the congregation stood up and ministered to us in song. I was totally captivated by their lovely voices and the heavenly music when a scuffle at the front door, to the left of the stage, drew the attention of many.

I ignored the noise and wished that people would be more considerate when entering during the service. Why couldn't they wait until the song item was over?

When I saw a man with a rifle standing in the doorway, I thought, "I wonder if this is the play that is to be presented to the young people tonight?"

The chaotic scene that was unfolding was no play; it was serious and incredibly real. Grenades were exploding in flashes of light. Pews shattered under the blasts, sending splinters flying through the air. An automatic assault rifle was being fired and was fast ripping the pews—and whoever, whatever was in its trajectory—to pieces. We were being attacked!

Instinctively, I knelt down behind the bench in front of me and pulled out my .38 Special snub-nosed revolver, which I always carried with me. I would have felt undressed without it. Many people could not understand why I would carry a firearm into a church service, but I argued that this was a particularly dangerous time in South Africa.

It was common knowledge that cars on the freeway, on which I travelled every day, were being stoned, not only causing damage to those cars, but also causing accidents. People were being terrorised, hijacked, murdered, and all in the name of fighting a just cause.

Well, my moment of truth had arrived, I thought, as my hands steadied around the revolver. The congregation had thrown themselves down—in order to protect themselves as far as possible from the deluge of flying bullets and shrapnel. By God's grace, the view of the terrorists from my seat, fourth row from the back of the church, was perfect. The building was built like a cinema with the floor sloping towards the stage in front. So without any hesitation, I knelt and aimed, firing two shots at the attackers. This appeared ineffective, as my position was too far from my targets to take precise aim with a snub-nosed revolver. I had to get closer to the terrorists.

So I started moving to the end of the pew on my haunches and leopard crawled the rest of the way when I realised that my position was too high up. The only way I could make those heartless thugs stop their vicious attack was to try and move in behind them and then shoot them in the back at close range.

I sprinted to the back door of the church, pushing a lady out of the way, so that I could kick the door open and not be hindered as I sought to get behind the gunmen to neutralise their attack.

As I desperately rounded the corner of the building, outside in the parking area, I saw a man standing next to what was the "getaway" car. Resting on his hip was his automatic rifle. He had it pointed up to the heavens, as if in defiance of the Lordship of Jesus Christ!

The man was looking in the direction of the door through which they had launched their attack. Was he waiting for people who would make easy targets to come running out, or maybe even for me?

I stepped back behind the corner of the wall and prepared to blast the last of my firepower. I strode out in full view of the terrorist and shot my last three rounds. By this time, the others were already in the car. My target jumped into the vehicle and the driver sped away immediately, leaving behind the acrid stench of burning tyres and exhaust fumes.

It's hard to express my feelings as I watched them drive away, but I remember thinking, "Lord why haven't I got more ammunition? Why? Why? Why?"

I ran across the road to the house of a neighbour and jumped over the fence. Knocking on the door, I shouted, "Call the police, there's been an attack!"

CHAPTER TWO

AFTERMATH

I RAN BACK into the church, using the same entrance that the terrorists had used. Not thinking that as I was still clutching my revolver, I could have been mistaken for a terrorist!

The overpowering stench of burnt gunpowder hung suspended in the air as dazed worshippers groped about on their hands and knees in search of loved ones amid the debris and sprawled, motionless bodies. Pools of freshly spilled blood trickled over the rich, blue carpets. The uncanny silence was punctuated with sobs and moans. Leaflets and Bibles were strewn about and a gaping hole in the floor bore evidence where a grenade had exploded.

I felt devastated and an immense sense of sadness. My emotions gave birth to a deep anger towards those people who could perpetrate such evil.

Though still in shock, the uninjured helped the injured. So I got busy, assisting wherever I could. Some people needed first aid for scrapes where shrapnel had hit them, while others with more serious injuries had to be helped onto stretchers and carried out to the ambulances that had arrived on the scene.

I ran over to the Children's Centre where a special programme for the children had been taking place. The little children were terrified. They were screaming in their panic, not understanding why their church, a safe place, had been attacked. I had to tell one of my friends, who had been helping with the children, that a nail was embedded in his wife's foot.

The attackers had attached nails to the outside of the hand grenades so that they had more impact on explosion.

I walked back into the church and continued assisting the injured. Finally I took a friend of one of the wounded to Groote Schuur Hospital. The injured girl's name was Gillian Schermbrucker. She was 19 years old and a medical student. We didn't know what to expect as a piece of shrapnel had pierced her lung.

I drove like a madman in my little *bakkie*. I was fired with rage and nervous energy. The young man suggested that I drive slower since there was no longer any need to rush at that stage.

After the hospital, I went to my sister's house where I was staying at the time. She wasn't home, so I went to my parents' house. I was still so filled with adrenalin that I remember bending the house key in the lock of the front door as I struggled to get the door open. Bending the key was something I probably would not be able to do under normal circumstances!

My entire family was gathered at my parents' home. I sat down with them in the family room, my wet, bloodstained clothes sticking to my body. I asked my father to pray. He thanked the Lord for His saving grace and hand on me during the attack and also prayed for the wounded and families of the deceased.

By then telephone calls had already started filtering in from around the country—from friends and family who wanted to know whether my parents and I were still alive. My parents usually go to church on a Sunday evening, but for some reason, they did not attend that night. A grenade had landed very close to where they normally sat.

AFTERMATH

I remember certain of the events of that evening first hand, and others I read in the press, or was told by friends. The local newspapers covered the massacre extensively over the next few days as the country reeled at the evil that had been unleashed that night. As news of the horror spread across the globe, churches everywhere prayed for the St James congregation and for the future of our country.

CHAPTER THREE

SHATTERED LIVES

ELEVEN PEOPLE had died and 53 were wounded. The injuries were horrendous, limbs were blown off and shrapnel and nails pierced defenceless bodies, killing or maiming worshipers.

Gerard Harker, a young man aged 21, was killed when he threw himself on top of one of the grenades. His body absorbed most of the blast and the police said that his act of bravery saved many lives. Unfortunately his younger brother, Wesley, aged 13, also did not escape the attack and he too died.

Richard O'Kill, a matric pupil of 17, threw himself across two young girls, shielding them from the bullet which struck him in the head—killing him instantly. He was to have joined his parents, who had emigrated to the United Kingdom, once he had completed his schooling later that year.

Marita Ackerman was sitting in the front of the church with visiting Russian seamen. She was shot in the chest and died 30 minutes after she arrived at the hospital. Her husband had seen a Russian friend on the other side of the church and had gone to sit with him. She left behind her husband and three children, two of whom had accompanied their parents to church that evening.

Marita had helped to start an outreach ministry for Russian seamen visiting Cape Town about two years previously. They would be fetched by bus and brought to the service. Afterwards, they would leave the church to go into a hall, where the Gospel message would be interpreted for them.

Four Russian seamen also lost their lives in the attack that night. They were: Valentin Varaksa, Andrei Kajil, Pavel Valujev and Oleg Karamzin.

Myrtle Smith's husband, Lorenzo, clutched his dying wife in his arms. A piece of shrapnel had pierced her heart. Myrtle was survived by Lorenzo and their two children.

Peter Gordon was another man who lost his wife that night. Denise Gordon died in hospital and Peter was wounded in the attack. Denise's young daughter was left without a mother.

Guy Javens died next to his wife of 10 years in the church. He had crouched down on his haunches when the attack started, but Marilyn, his bewildered wife, noticed that he was still crouched and that he did not answer her when she called to him once it was over. An usher confirmed that he had died during the attack.

Dimitri Makagon, a Ukrainian seaman, was one of the worst injured in the attack. A grenade fell into his lap and both his legs were ripped off. His right arm had to be amputated and the doctors feared that he would not live. He was 23 and earning money as a sailor to pay for his wedding on his return home to his fiancée.

Dimitri survived and his fiancée came out to South Africa and they were later married by Bishop Frank Retief, the Rector of St James Church. They were living in Cape Town at the time of writing.

Gillian Schermbrucker, the plucky medical student who had been so badly injured, also survived the attack.

CHAPTER FOUR

THE NEXT DAY

THE POLICE CALLED me in the day after the attack. They had established their headquarters, for the purpose of the investigation, on the church premises. I met the generals, who congratulated me for returning fire. I had to explain in detail everything that had taken place the previous evening to the head of the Murder and Robbery Squad.

The police officers were exhausted and had had little or no sleep the previous night. After giving a statement to an officer I spent some time walking around the church, reliving the massacre. An officer showed me where my one round had imbedded itself into the wall, but he was concerned that there was no sign of the other round fired in the church.

I was overcome with worry as it was explained to me that if I had hit a parishioner and killed him or her, I would have to face a charge of culpable homicide. They did not find the round and it was later discovered that it had been that bullet which had hit one of the terrorists.

I felt that the best way for me to cope with the attack and the worry that I may have unintentionally harmed an innocent person was to return to work. At the time, I was working as an insurance assessor for my father.

After speaking to the police, I met with a client, who lived a short distance from Cape Town. My client asked me if I had heard about the attack of the previous night. He went on to tell me about the young man who had shot back and he said that he believed that many more people would have been killed if it were not for the unknown man's actions. I just nodded that I had heard about the attack.

That evening, some friends and I went to a political rally held by the Freedom Front, a conservative political party headed by an ex-military general, Constand Viljoen. We were there to hand out leaflets and newsletters for Africa Christian Action, Frontline Fellowship and United Christian Action, organisations with which I was involved. These organisations attempted to give a Biblical response to the challenges facing the country.

I was asked to help somebody carry a table from an enclosed area into the foyer. When we entered the area, I saw General Viljoen standing there and we started speaking about the church massacre of the night before. He said that he was unhappy about what had happened and also mentioned it in his speech.

The proceedings started with a reading from the Bible and prayer. During the prayer, I could hear some Afrikaners laughing and joking in the foyer where I was standing looking after the literature table. Their disrespect for God infuriated me.

"Why did I even bother trying to save lives last night? This country deserves the government they get," I thought to myself.

Different thoughts flashed through my mind. I could not understand why the Afrikaners had fallen so low as to forsake God, whom their forefathers had worshipped and feared. The Afrikaners had been neutralised and had been manipulated by the media into thinking that they were the cause of all that was evil in South Africa.

THE NEXT DAY

I could not handle the laughing and whispering during the prayers any longer. I told my friend Peter Hammond, Director and Founder of Frontline Fellowship, that I was leaving and then I walked out.

CHAPTER FIVE

THE TRAUMA HITS

I SAT IN MY CAR outside my sister's house. It was then that the trauma of the night before hit me. I started shaking and sobbing. I could not stop. The tears rolled down my cheeks as I asked the Lord why He had not given me the privilege of killing just one of those terrorists? Why had I missed?

Maybe if I had reacted faster, those husbands would not have lost their wives, parents their children and others their loved ones! I felt that it was my fault that all those people's lives had been lost. Yes, in my post-shooting trauma, I had forgotten the sovereignty of God.

I went into my sister's house and found her in the kitchen, where she was busy cleaning. I leant against the stove and looked at her. "Why didn't I blow those bastards' brains out?" I asked her desperately.

The tears were still streaming down my face. Although I don't remember her exact answer, it would have been wise. She is a godly woman whose strength and Christian walk has been an example to many.

A few days later my Aunt Averil phoned; she insisted that I go to the debriefing sessions being held by the police psychologists. They were specially trained to help people cope with traumatic incidents of crime in their lives. She probably knew that without her prompting, I wouldn't go near a psychologist. I felt that I had to listen to her; after all she had helped to teach me to walk!

I rounded up some friends, as there was no way I was going to a *kop krapper* session alone. We arrived at the meeting in the Children's Centre at the church. Chairs had been placed in a circle and people were seated, waiting for the meeting to begin.

The psychologist was a young man in his late twenties who introduced himself and then asked each of us to do the same. There were 25 of us seated. I am not the most patient person and the thought of each of us having to give answers to the same questions 25 times dismayed me. "I don't want to hear all these peoples' problems," I thought to myself.

I discovered that I was going through the same post-traumatic stress as the rest of the group, namely, intermittent headaches, excessive sweating, concern about being followed and jumping whenever I heard a loud noise. I was concerned with my own selfishness as I pondered these thoughts.

Eventually we reached a stage where we had to talk about how we felt about the attack and also our thoughts on the terrorists themselves.

I was in a group with the entire family of one of the deceased. Her husband explained how he had covered his wife with his body as the attack started. A piece of shrapnel from a hand grenade had passed through the sleeve of his jacket, missed his arm, passed through the other side of his sleeve and pierced her lungs. She had later died in the hospital. I was shocked when her daughter said she had forgiven the terrorists for murdering her mother. Meeting this family made a huge impact on my life. After the session I just walked up to the father and hugged him. What else could I do?

I thought differently to the rest of the group and expressed my real feelings when the time came. I hated the terrorists with all my being. This was of course an unbiblical stand, but I was not going to lie. I said exactly what I had felt!

Cara, a friend of mine who was in the group, said that when she heard me say this, she just thought to herself, "Oh no, Charl, just please keep quiet rather!"

A lady in the group tried to console me by saying, "Imagine how you would have felt if you had killed one of the terrorists!"

I said nothing because frankly, I would have felt great. What is wrong with defending the innocent with lethal force? However, I must stress that I did not plan to hunt down the attackers and make them pay for what they had done. I believe that justice lies in the hands of the judicial authority here on earth and that ultimately, we are all answerable to a higher authority.

CHAPTER SIX

OUTRAGE

POLITICIANS CLAMOURED to express their indignation at the attack. It seemed as if they gained points for the more horror they expressed. No organisation was willing to claim responsibility for this heinous act.

Even the organisation that was later found to be responsible went on record to deny any involvement. They did, however, suggest that the only reason that the media had devoted so much space and attention to the massacre was because most of the victims were white.

This was a very unfair accusation, as St James prided itself on being a non-racial congregation made up of members from all population groups.

I first came to the attention of the media because of the colour of my skin. Survivors of the attack reported that at least one of the gunmen was white. The police then cleared the confusion by releasing my identity to the press. It was further explained that I had returned fire, chased after the attackers and fired shots at their car.

Imagine my shock on the morning of Tuesday 27 July 1993 when on opening the *Cape Times* newspaper, I read the following: "Archbishop Desmond Tutu said yesterday he did not believe churchgoers should allow themselves to use the same methods (guns) as those evil people. One must remember that the Bible says, 'Vengeance is mine, sayeth the Lord.'"

The Archbishop did not differentiate between "defence of the innocent" and "taking of revenge." I had tried to protect innocent brothers and sisters in Christ from murderers and not taken revenge by following the terrorists and killing them days later.

The media quickly honed in on the debate. For the most part, I was strongly lauded by many people who thought that by returning fire I had prevented further carnage. I well believe that the terrorists never expected a benign target, like a churchgoer, to retaliate.

Both friends and strangers supported me by writing to the newspapers and telephoning radio stations to express their approval of my reaction. I am very thankful that there were so many concerned people who reassured me of the integrity of my actions.

PART TWO

CHAPTER SEVEN

MILITARY TRAINING

"IF ONE of your troops shows cowardice in the face of the enemy and runs away during a contact, then you shoot him in the back as he flees!"

We were being lectured by our captain during training at the Infantry School, a military academy in South Africa that trained commissioned and non-commissioned officers for duty in the Defence Force.

Before the African National Congress (ANC) came into power, all white South African men had to offer up two years of their lives to serve their country in the military or some other institution of the government's choice. As happens in armies across the world, the training breaks the spirits of some men while it brings out the best in others.

Most people know that during basic training, the aim of those in authority is to totally break your confidence, and then to mould you into a disciplined soldier who will act with precision and courage on the battlefield. Under extreme provocation or in a war situation, we are taught to act fast, with purpose and without hesitation. At the time of going through so many ridiculous and sadistic drills, I could never have imagined them being of any use to me in my "life after the army," yet they stood me in good stead during the massacre.

I decided to join the Infantry with the aim of becoming an officer. They took us in and put us through a sifting period of six weeks after which we were posted to the Infantry School.

It goes without saying that I hated the Infantry. Everything was geared to wasting our time, to putting us through mental strain and just frustrating us totally. Meanwhile they watched us closely to see how we handled things.

One day we came back from a long march to find our cupboards completely trashed. This was after it had taken us hours to arrange everything in the neatest, straightest way—army fashion. In fact we had left everything this way for weeks! A corporal had come along and thrown all the clothes out, put shaving cream on everything and had caused utter chaos. I remember a fellow student cracking up, shouting and generally venting his frustration. The best way for me to handle the situation was simply to laugh.

On one occasion after taking too long to fetch our coffee, our platoon sergeant took our coffee and threw it all out in the gutter. Thirsty from the morning's physical training, we could only stand by and watch. I really missed the comfort of my mother's kitchen at such times and was very grateful for the food packages she sent me.

On another occasion when we were inspected by the platoon sergeant, he discovered that our coffee canister had not been emptied and washed. This time he emptied the contents of the canister on our beautifully polished floor, a floor in which you could see your face as clearly as if looking into a mirror.

What lessons we had to learn in cleanliness, discipline, patience, as well as forgiveness for the platoon sergeant. We had to learn how to endure hardships so that instead of being on the verge of a breakdown all the time, we would be calm and deliberate.

There were times when I questioned the Lord, asking Him why He had pushed me into this situation. Yet I knew the answer. He has pushed and nudged me many times in my life, into areas I did not always like, but instead of sitting around and praying that the Lord would lead me, and doing nothing about it myself, I would go out and do the job.

The Lord often pushes us into areas we might not want to enter. Then, when we are obedient, we find we are in the right place at the right time.

We did a lot of bush work as part of our Infantry training. This was done in the Oudtshoorn area in the Western Cape, where we would stay out for weeks in the field in the freezing cold. Here we were trained to handle surprise attacks from the enemy.

Certain manoeuvres were so drilled into our heads that we could have carried them out in our sleep. One set of commands was: dash, down, crawl, roll, observe, sights, fire. If we saw the "enemy," we would have to dash towards any available cover, for example, an anthill, go down before we got to cover, crawl towards cover, then roll into the cover, observe where the enemy was—from behind the cover, put our sights on them and fire back at them. These words: dash, down, crawl, roll, observe, sights, fire—were so imprinted on our brains and we were so wired up, we would not have thought twice about following through if we came across the enemy. This was the exact drill that I used when the church came under attack.

A rapid and correct response was demanded from officers. There was no time to discuss, or ask for a "democratic show of hands" if we expected to hit the enemy in the bush. We were also taught that we were NEVER to retreat when in a contact. Even if our men were being wiped out, we were not to retreat, maybe because this was a bush war and not conventional warfare.

The only time we could move backwards was if we were to attack the enemy from a different angle. This was called "fire and movement," so we would stop, shoot and move forward, stop, shoot and move forward in battle formation again and again for as many times as this was needed.

The infantry made disciplined soldiers out of us. We became very aggressive; we were under a great deal of stress. As officers, our own lives were at higher risk, as the enemy would go for soldiers with rank first. If the leaders were wiped out, it would be easier to wipe out the rest of the men. Our lives had to be sacrificed before the lives of our men. For instance if a grenade was thrown and threatened the lives of our platoon, we were to throw ourselves onto it to save our men.

In my second year when I had received my commission as a second lieutenant, I used to drive around in the Eastern Cape with Staff Sergeant "Pepsi" Pretorius. He normally drove, while I relaxed—a condition that suited us both.

The reason I mention him is because while we were travelling along mountain passes and the mountainside, he would continually be on the lookout for where he could place his LMG (light machine gun).

The LMG weighed about 12 kilograms and had to be carried up onto a hill to provide fire cover for the troops during an attack. He was constantly thinking ahead about where to place the LMG to give the best advantage to the troops. Eventually I started to think ahead in the same way; no matter where I was, I was always planning my strategy either in a defensive or an offensive way. It is strange that this thinking ahead stayed with me even after I had completed my two years in the army. I can remember sitting in the church near my parents and wondering what I would do, where I would go, if the church were attacked. By the time it actually happened I'd already thought through exactly what I would do!

Another aspect of our training I should mention is the spiritual side. Something that Americans found very interesting when I was there was that we were forced to worship God in the army. In fact they were stunned.

We had to have two "quiet times" a day, 15 minutes in the morning and 10 minutes in the evening. We had to sit on our *trommels*, read our Bibles and pray. If we dared read any other book we would be in major trouble.

We also had prayer parades from time to time, where the officer on duty would read the Bible and pray. The same applied to all official parades. There were always ministers on the border to give us spiritual help. My time in the Infantry was a time of great spiritual growth for me.

It is amazing how few atheists there are to be found in a war zone. I made some very good friends in the army, who have remained my friends ever since. There might be thousands of people in your base but you could still get lonely. This is where brothers in Christ played a large part in giving each other prayer and general support as we went through some very hard times together. One of my friends, who had done his training before me, told me that if I had never learnt to pray before, I would do so in the army. I have always marvelled at how true this was.

While doing my army training, I did not understand the Biblical principles of self-defence or of war. I remember thinking that I wouldn't like to get into an attack situation where I'd have to kill anyone. This was until I understood the principles laid down in Scripture for self-defence and for fighting in a war situation. Now I would not have a problem at all.

I saw my defence of the South West African (now Namibian) border as part of my duty to the nation. I had no problem fighting communists. They were anti-God and a threat to the Church. At no time was it ever found that they had any leanings towards biblical principles or a life of communion with Jesus Christ; this was gathered from the prisoners of war that were taken.

According to *The Black Book of Communism* by Courtois *et al*, nearly 100 million people had been murdered by communists between 1917 and 1991.

We were also trained to protect South Africa's interests in South West Africa (Namibia). South West Africa was awarded to South Africa as a protectorate after the First World War by the League of Nations. We were stationed in the northern areas protecting the country from a communist/socialist invasion by the South West African forces of SWAPO.

Cuban forces were called in by the Angolan government to fight on the side of SWAPO and also to wipe out UNITA in the south of Angola. UNITA was a democratic freedom fighting organisation that was anti-communist and as such, a threat to the communist government of Angola.

Infantry school called on us to endure rigorous training before being sent up to northern Namibia where we would train in the line of fire. I often wondered how anyone could survive up there without the benefit of training at infantry school.

The whole point of our training was for us to overcome our most basic fears so that we could function—no matter what sort of pressures or circumstances we would face in our future duties. The physical, mental and emotional stress they put us under defies description. We went for days with little food and little sleep.

I can remember our platoon sleeping in muddy trenches, running through dirty water, crawling under barbed wire and jumping over high fences—all with our full kit on. Other times we went on forced marches of endless miles, running with large poles on our shoulders that caused our feet to blister. The pain was indescribable. As soon as we thought that we were nearing the end of the agony, a corporal would yell at us to carry on.

We learnt a lesson through all of this. We could survive with little sleep and we could survive with little food. We proved to ourselves that we could do what we had to do. It just goes to show that the limits of a man are way beyond what we would normally imagine.

CHAPTER EIGHT

SPIRITUAL PREPARATION

D URING my second year in the army I came to hear about an organisation called Frontline Fellowship. I used to watch school rugby with a teacher friend of mine who, while we were chatting, happened to mention a group of crazy people — ex-soldiers, mad missionaries, who were working in this organisation. They would undertake cross border evangelism into communist countries around us, showing no fear of attacks and at great risk of being killed. Some even served time in jail. This intrigued me. I thought that I would look them up sometime.

I believe by the Lord's leading, while visiting Jonathan Cameron, a friend of mine, I came across a booklet in his house from Frontline Fellowship. The booklet was called *The Christian at War* and was written by Reverend Peter Hammond. It was brilliant, setting out the Biblical principles of war — not spiritual warfare but actual physical warfare showing Christians under which circumstances they could fight.

What I read really excited me. This was the first time I had come across such a clear and concise account of all the Biblical principles I needed in order to understand the quandary I was finding myself in. I met with Peter Hammond and went into training under him. Since then he has become my mentor and a good family friend.

It is a sad fact that so many of us hear awful stories and read horror reports in newspapers and after the initial shock, just go on with our lives and are totally unaffected by them. It always takes personal experience of the horror of crime out there before we act. My personal experiences not only affected me, but also played a huge part in my going out and buying a gun.

A friend and I were driving towards Wellington one night. We were on our way to look after his parents' farm while they were away. We were in a *bakkie*, nearing the outskirts of Wellington, when we saw a fire in the road. We carried on towards it and realised that there were people standing nearby— around someone or something.

I slowed down and saw it was a tyre burning. The next thing we knew, we were bombarded with bricks and stones. I did a quick U-turn; my adrenaline pumping and emotions mixed with fear and rage, I drove straight to the police station to report the incident. The police took off immediately to deal with the situation. Only then did we take the time to assess the damage.

There was no doubt in my mind that the Lord had had His hand on us that night. One of the bricks missed my friend's head by two and a half centimetres when it was thrown at his window. It hit the metal body of the vehicle instead. Another brick, which should have come directly through the windscreen and would have hit me full on, actually bounced off the windscreen wiper and only managed to crack the window.

This was when I made the decision to buy a firearm. The next time anyone threatened my life by throwing a brick at me, I was going to shoot back! Within two weeks, I had a firearm; it was much quicker to get a licence in those days. Having bought the firearm I had a difficult decision to make: when to carry it, and when to use it.

SPIRITUAL PREPARATION

Theologically, there is a big difference between going to war on behalf of a constitutional authority where you are expected to carry and use a firearm and carrying one in your personal capacity and deciding for yourself under which circumstances to use it. Not surprisingly, I was conflicted—I wanted to make the correct decision in the Biblical manner.

CHAPTER NINE

FINDING ANSWERS

IT WAS ONLY AFTER reading *The Biblical Principles of Gun Control* by Larry Pratt, the president of Gun Owners of America, that I realised there was no problem whatsoever for Christians to be involved in self-defence and the protection of their families.

Reading this article was like an answer to a prayer. All at once I had found answers to all the questions that had been plaguing me. I am sure that the arguments put forward by Larry would help anybody who is experiencing the same kind of doubt. So, with Larry's permission, I have included the article in its entirety below:

What does the Bible say about gun control?

The underlying argument for gun control seems to be that the availability of guns causes crime. By extension, the availability of any weapon would have to be viewed as a cause of crime. What does the Bible say about such a view?

Perhaps we should start at the beginning, or at least very close to the beginning—in Genesis 4. In this chapter we read about the first murder. Cain had offered an unacceptable sacrifice, and Cain was upset that God insisted that he do the right thing. In other words, Cain was peeved that he could not do his own thing.

Cain decided to kill his brother rather than get right with God. There were no guns available, although there may well have been a knife. Whether it was a knife or a rock, the Bible does not say. The point is; the evil in Cain's heart was the cause of the murder, not the availability of the murder weapon.

God's response was not to ban rocks or knives, or whatever, but to banish the murderer. Later (see Genesis 9:5-6), God instituted capital punishment, but said not a word about banning weapons.

Did Christ teach pacifism?

Many people, Christians included, assume that Christ taught pacifism. They recite Matthew 5:38-39 for their proof. In this verse Christ said: "You have heard that it was said, an eye for an eye and a tooth for a tooth. But I tell you not to resist an evil person. But whoever slaps you on your right cheek, turn the other to him also."

The Sermon on the Mount, from which this passage is taken, deals with righteous personal conduct. In our passage, Christ is clearing up a confusion that had led people to think that conduct proper for the civil government—that is, taking vengeance—was also proper for an individual.

Even the choice of words used by Christ indicates that He was addressing a confusion, or a distortion, that was commonplace. Several times in the rest of the Sermon on the Mount, Christ used this same "you have heard it said" figure of speech to straighten out misunderstandings or falsehoods being taught by the religious leaders of the times. Contrast this to Christ's use of the phrase "it is written" when He was appealing to the Scriptures for authority (for example, see Matthew 4, where on three occasions during His temptation by the devil, Christ answered each one of the devil's lies or misquotes from Scripture with the words: "it is written").

To further underscore the point that Christ was correcting the religious leaders on their teaching that "an eye for an eye" applies to private revenge, consider that in the same Sermon, Christ strongly condemned false teaching: "Whoever therefore breaks one of the commandments, and teaches men so, shall be called least in the kingdom of heaven..." (Matthew 5:19) Clearly, then, Christ was not teaching something different about self-defence from that which is taught elsewhere in the Bible. Otherwise, He would be contradicting Himself for He would then be teaching men to break one of the commandments.

The Bible distinguishes clearly between the duties of the civil magistrate (the government) and the duties of an individual. Namely, God had delegated to the civil magistrate the administration of justice. Individuals have the responsibility of protecting their lives from attackers. Christ was referring to this distinction in the Matthew 5 passage. Let us now examine in some detail what the Scriptures say about the roles of government and of individuals.

Both the Old and New Testaments teach individual self-defence, even if it means taking the assailant's life in certain circumstances.

Self-defence in the Old Testament

Exodus 22:2-3 tells us: "If the thief is found breaking in, and he is struck so that he dies, there shall be no guilt for his bloodshed. If the sun has risen on him, there shall be guilt for his bloodshed. He should make full restitution; if he has nothing, then he shall be sold for his theft."

One conclusion to draw from this is that a threat to our life is to be met with lethal force. During the day, presumably because we can recognise and later apprehend the thief if he escapes, we are not to kill him in non-life-threatening circumstances.

In Proverbs 25:26 we read: "A righteous man who falters before the wicked is like a murky spring and a polluted well." Certainly, we would be faltering before the wicked if we chose to be unarmed and unable to resist an assailant who might be threatening our life.

Role of government

Resisting an attack is not to be confused with taking vengeance, which is the exclusive domain of God (Romans 12:19). This has been delegated to the civil magistrate, who, as we read in Romans 13:4, "...is God's minister to you for good. But if you do evil, be afraid; for he does not bear the sword in vain; for he is God's minister, an avenger to execute wrath on him who practices evil."

Private vengeance means one would stalk down a criminal after one's life is no longer in danger as opposed to defending oneself during an attack. It is this very point that has been confused by Christian pacifists who would take the passage in the Sermon on the Mount about turning the other cheek (which prohibits private vengeance) into a command to falter before the wicked.

Let us consider also, that the Sixth Commandment tells us: "Thou shall not murder." In the chapters following, God gave to Moses many of the situations that require a death penalty. God clearly has not told us never to kill. He has told us not to murder, which means we are not to take an innocent life.

Self-defence in the New Testament

The Christian pacifist may try to argue that God has changed His mind from the time that He gave Moses the Ten Commandments on Mount Sinai. Perhaps they want us to think that Christ cancelled out the Ten Commandments in Exodus 20 or the provision for justifiably killing a thief in Exodus 22. But the writer of Hebrews made it clear that this cannot be, because "Jesus Christ is the same yesterday, today and forever." (Hebrews 13:8) In the Old Testament, the prophet Malachi records God's words this way: "For I am the Lord, I do not change." (Malachi 3:6)

Paul was referring to the unchangeability of God's Word when he wrote to Timothy: "All Scripture is given by inspiration of God, and is profitable for doctrine, for reproof, for correction, for instruction in righteousness, that the man of God may be complete, thoroughly equipped for every good work." (2 Timothy 3:16-17) Clearly, Paul viewed all Scripture, including the Old Testament, as useful for training Christians in every area of life.

We must also consider what Christ told his disciples during his last hours with them: "...But now, he who has a money bag, let him take it, and likewise a sack; and he who has no sword, let him sell his garment and buy one." (Luke 22:36) Keep in mind that the sword was the finest offensive weapon available to an individual soldier—the equivalent then of a military assault rifle today.

The Christian pacifist will likely object at this point that only a few hours later, Christ rebuked Peter who used a sword to cut off the ear of Malchus, a servant of the high priest in the company of a detachment of troops. Let us read what Christ said to Peter in Matthew 26:52-54: "Put your sword in its place, for all who take the sword will perish by the sword. Or do you think that I cannot now pray to My Father, and He will provide Me with more than twelve legions of angels. How then could the Scriptures be fulfilled, that it must happen thus?"

It was not the first time that Christ had to explain to the disciples why He had come to earth. To fulfil the Scriptures, the Son of God had to die for the sin of man—since man was incapable of paying for his own sin apart from going to hell. Christ could have saved His life, but then believers would have lost their lives forever in hell. These things only became clear to the disciples after Christ had died and been raised from the dead and the Spirit had come into the world at Pentecost (see John 14:26).

While Christ told Peter to "put your sword in its place," He clearly did not say, "get rid of it forever." That would have contradicted what he had told the disciples only hours before. Peter's sword was to protect his own mortal life from danger. His sword was not needed to protect the Creator of the Universe and the King of kings.

Years after Pentecost, Paul wrote in a letter to Timothy, "But if anyone does not provide for his own, and especially of those of his household, he has denied the faith and is worse than an unbeliever." (1 Timothy 5:8) This passage applies to our subject because it would be absurd to buy a house, furnish it with food and facilities for one's family, and then refuse to install locks and provide the means to protect the family and the property. Likewise it would be absurd not to take, if necessary, the life of a night-time thief to protect the members of the family (see Exodus 22:2-3).

A related and even broader concept is found in the parable of the Good Samaritan. Christ had referred to the Old Testament summary of all the Laws of the Bible into two great commandments: "'You shall love the Lord your God with all your heart, with all your soul, with all your strength, and with all your mind,' and 'your neighbour as yourself'" (Luke 10:27).

When asked who was a neighbour, Christ related the parable of the Good Samaritan (Luke 10:30-37). It was the Good Samaritan who took care of the mugging victim who was a neighbour to the victim. The others who walked by and ignored the victim's plight were not acting as neighbours to him.

In the light of all we have seen the Scriptures teach to this point, can we argue that if we were able to save another's life by shooting an attacker with our firearm—that we should "turn the other cheek" instead? The Bible speaks of no such right. It only speaks of our responsibilities in the face of an attack—as individual creatures made by God, as householders or as neighbours.

National blessings and cursings

The Old Testament also tells us a great deal about the positive relationship between righteousness, which exalts a nation, and self-defence.

It makes clear that in times of national rebellion against the Lord God, the rulers of the nation will reflect the spiritual degradation of the people and the result is a denial of God's commandments, an arrogance of officialdom, disarmament and oppression.

For example, the people of Israel were oppressed during the time of the rule of the Judges. This occurred every time the people apostatised. Judges 5:8 tells us: "They chose new gods; when there was war in the gates; not a shield or spear was seen among forty thousand in Israel."

Consider Israel under Saul: the first book of Samuel tells of Israel's turning away from God. The people did not want to be governed by God; they wanted to be ruled by a king like the pagan, God-hating nations around them. Samuel warned the people what they were getting into—the curses that would be upon them—if they persisted in raising up a king over themselves. Included in those curses was the raising up of a standing, professional army, which would take their sons and their daughters for aggressive wars (1 Samuel 8:11-13).

This curse is not unknown in the USA. Saul carried out all the judgements that Samuel had warned the people about. His building up of a standing army has been repeated in the USA, and not just in terms of the military, but also the 650,000 full-time police officers from all levels of government.

Saul was the king the Israelites wanted and got. He was beautiful in the eyes of the world but a disaster in the eyes of the Lord. Saul did not trust God; he rebelled against His mandates. On the evening of one battle, when the prophet Samuel was to come and perform a sacrifice unto the Lord, Saul put himself above God; he was impatient. He refused to wait for Samuel because God's way was taking too long. Saul went ahead and performed the sacrifice himself, thus violating God's commandment (and, incidentally, also violating the God-ordained separation of duties of church and state)!

Thus was the kingdom lost to Saul. And it was under him that the Philistines were able to defeat the Jews and put them into bondage. So great was the bondage exerted by the Philistines that, "Now there was no blacksmith to be found throughout all the land of Israel: for the Philistines said, 'lest the Hebrews made them swords or spears.' But all the Israelites went down to the Philistines to sharpen each man's ploughshare, his mattock, his axe, and his sickle; ... So it came about, on the day of battle, that there was neither sword nor spear found in the hand of any of the people who were with Saul and Jonathan..." (1 Samuel 13:19-20, 22-23)

Today, the same goals of the Philistines would be carried out by an oppressor who would ban gunsmiths from the land. The sword of today is the handgun, rifle or shotgun. The sword control of the Philistines is today's gun control of those governments that do not trust their people with guns.

It is important to understand that what happened to the Jews at the time of Saul was not unexpected according to the sanctions spelled out by God in Leviticus 26 and Deuteronomy 28. In the first verses of those chapters, blessings are promised to a nation that keeps God's laws. In the second parts of those chapters, curses are spelled out for a nation that rebels against God. Deuteronomy 28:47-48 helps us understand the reason for Israel's oppression by the Philistines during Saul's reign: "Because you did not serve the Lord your God with joy and gladness of heart, for the abundance of all things, therefore you shall serve your enemies, whom the Lord will send against you, in hunger, in thirst, in nakedness, and in need of all things; and

He will put a yoke of iron on your neck until He has destroyed you."

The Bible provides examples of God's blessing on Israel for its faithfulness. These blessings included a strong national defence coupled with peace. A clear example occurred during the reign of Jehoshaphat. Second Chronicles 17 tells of how Jehoshaphat led Israel back to faithfulness to God—which included a strong national defence. The result: "And the fear of the Lord fell on all the kingdoms of the lands that were around Judah, so that they did not make war against Jehoshaphat." (2 Chronicles 17:10)

The Israelite army was a militia army, which came to battle with each man bearing his own weapons— from the time of Moses, through the Judges, and beyond. When threatened by the Midianites, for example, "So Moses spoke to the people saying, 'Arm yourselves for the war, and let them go against the Midianites to take vengeance for the Lord on Midian.'" (Numbers 31:3)

Again, to demonstrate the Biblical heritage of individuals bearing and keeping arms, during David's time in the wilderness avoiding capture by Saul, "David said to his men, 'Every man gird on his sword.' So every man girded on his sword, and David also girded on his sword." (1 Samuel 25:13)

Finally, consider Nehemiah and those who rebuilt the gates and walls of Jerusalem. They were both builders and defenders, each man—each servant—armed with his own weapon: "Those who built on the wall, and those who carried burdens loaded themselves so that with one hand they worked a construction, and with the other held a weapon. Every one of the builders had his sword girded at his side as he built." (Nehemiah 4:17-18)

Conclusion

The wisdom of the framers of the American Constitution is consistent with the lessons of the Bible. Instruments of defence should be dispersed throughout the nation, not concentrated in the hands of the central government. In a godly country, righteousness governs each man through the Holy Spirit working within. The government has no cause to want a monopoly of force; the government that desires such a monopoly is a threat to the lives, liberty and property of its citizens.

The assumption that only danger can result from people carrying guns is used to justify government monopoly of force. The notion that the people cannot be trusted to keep and bear their own arms informs us that ours, like the time of Solomon, may be one of great riches but is also a time of peril to free people. If Christ is not our King, we shall have a dictator to rule over us, just as Samuel warned.

For those who think that God treated Israel differently from the way He will treat us today, please consider what God told the prophet Malachi: "For I am the Lord, I do not change..." (Malachi 3:6)

CHAPTER TEN

CHOOSING YOUR FIGHTS

MY FRIENDS and I believe firmly in the Biblical principles of self-defence, yet in certain circumstances, such as suffering for the cause of the Gospel, there are times when the use of a firearm would be totally inappropriate.

The best way to explain this statement is to mention some incidents in which my friends have been involved.

Johan van Zyl, my brother in Christ, was with Frontline Fellowship on a mission trip in Sudan. The aim of the mission was to hand out Bibles to the soldiers and to present them with the Gospel. At a military unit he was visiting, one of the soldiers, who happened to be their best soldier, challenged him to a fight. The soldier, armed with a sheathed knife, attacked Johan from behind. Before the soldier knew what had hit him, Johan had him pinned to the ground and turned the knife on him! This actually stood Johan in good stead, opening the way for him to share the Gospel with troops who now respected him. He and the soldier became good friends.

In contrast to this show of strength, Johan chose not to retaliate when he was attacked by a pimp, who broke his nose, while he was evangelising outside brothels in the city of Durban in South Africa.

Reverend Peter Hammond, Director of Frontline Fellowship, has had many experiences in which his life has been threatened. Certain circumstances required the use of a firearm and others not. Peter has been jailed in Zambia and Mozambique while evangelising in the war zones of Africa. He also had a pimp hold a revolver under his chin and threaten to "blow his brains out" if he carried on evangelising among his girls and prospective clients.

He realised that in the above instances, the use of force would be inappropriate. Yet when a young man approached him with a knife in his hand at a petrol station while he was filling his motorbike with gas and demanded that Peter get off the bike so that he could "annex" it, a simple brandishing of a firearm with a courteous, "Yes of course," persuaded the would-be thief to run away.

Albert Otter, another friend, chased and caught a thief, who had grabbed an old lady's handbag and ran off with it. When he caught the thief and tugged the handbag back, the thief pulled out a large knife to threaten Albert. Just then a shopkeeper came out of his shop with a pistol in his hand, pointed it at the thief and "suggested" that he leave Albert alone!

One afternoon, while driving home from work, my brother-in-law saw a motorist in a car that had a broken window chasing another car. He realised that the occupants of the car being chased had probably broken into the pursuing car. During the chase, the car in front crossed an island with bushes and drove into the oncoming traffic with the other car still in hot pursuit.

Meanwhile, my brother-in-law managed to race ahead and was next to the getaway car as it drove through the bushes on the island to reappear on the correct side of the road. He pulled out his 9mm pistol, pointed it at the occupants of the car and told them to pull over, which they did. He kept his firearm on them and had them lying on the road, spread-eagled, until the police arrived and recovered the stolen goods from the thieves. A large knife was found on one of the thieves who had tried to get close enough to use it on him after their car had stopped. The 9mm pistol had been an obvious deterrent.

John Brown, a missionary friend of mine—who works in the central African state of Sudan, where Christians in the South are being enslaved, persecuted and murdered by the largely Islamic north—was jailed in Zambia, Mozambique and Namibia while taking the Gospel into these areas. Yet not once, while being persecuted for the sake of the Gospel, did he find it necessary to use a firearm to defend himself.

PART THREE

CHAPTER ELEVEN

SPEAKING OUT

A FEW WEEKS AFTER what was by then known as the St James Massacre, I was invited by United Christian Action to speak at a seminar on the "Christian Response to the Terrorist Attack." The paper that I presented is reproduced below in its entirety:

> God has delegated punishment of the wicked to the Constitutional authorities and finally to Himself. I believe that defence of one's family and property must lie in the hands of the individual. Government agencies, like the police, cannot be everywhere at the same time, protecting the innocent.

> I believe that Christians do not only need to prepare themselves spiritually for any crisis in their lives, but also physically. We have to get out of thinking that these two important areas of our existence are totally separate. It is disgraceful that certain Christian men will nurture their families spiritually but when they are attacked, these same men will not lift a hand to protect their loved ones from disaster.

> In spiritual preparation it is important to move away from the weak, shallow gospel preached by some. We need to rediscover the Nature of God. He is all-

powerful, infinite, all-knowing, and is not a weak being Who is disinterested in our lives. We should be wary of only telling people that God loves them and that He has a wonderful plan for their lives. God hates the wicked and the only plan He has for their lives, if they don't come to repentance and faith in Him, is an eternity in hell. Why should we use deception in our evangelism?

Proverbs 9:10 teaches us: "The fear of the Lord is the beginning of wisdom." We need to obey His Law/Word. After all, He gave us the Scriptures for a reason. If we obey them, He will surely bless us. If we reject His Word, we can expect God's judgement to come upon us. We need to meditate on the Word of God day and night because "through the law we become conscious of sin" (Romans 3:20) and the "law of the Lord is perfect, converting the soul" (Psalm 19:7). "Sin is lawlessness" (1 John 3:4), so if we do not obey the Law of God in all areas of government assigned to man by God, which is self, family, church and state government, then we are in sin before our Lord.

Many speak of "accepting Christ as our Saviour." Is 'accepting' a Biblical term, or is it watered down from the truth? The Bible speaks of "repentance" (Acts 3:19), "turning to God" (Acts 26:20) and having "faith in our Lord Jesus" (Acts 20:21) and also that Christ is to be our "Lord and Saviour" (2 Peter 3:2). Why do we teach that Christ can be our Saviour but not Lord of our lives? Surely the two go together?

We need to understand the doctrine of eternal judgement, the wrath of God and the reality of hell. In Luke 12:4-5, Jesus taught: "Do not be afraid of those who kill the body and after that can do no more, but I will show you whom you should fear: fear Him who, after the killing of the body, has power to throw you into hell. Yes I tell you, fear God."

God is love but He is also a just God. He will make sure that justice is served, if not on earth then on Judgement Day.

Living in this sinful world, you need to be prepared to meet your maker. How is this done? First of all, we need to recognise that we are sinners before a righteous God who hates sin. We have to put our faith in Jesus Christ whose blood was shed on the cross on the hill called Calvary. You see, God demands that blood needs to be shed to make atonement for sin. This was done by His Son, Jesus Christ, so that those He calls will have their penalties paid for. We need to repent of all our sin and turn away from it and our Heavenly Father, who is righteous and just, will cleanse us of all our wickedness.

If we don't have life in Christ on earth then we are doomed to destruction in death. Christ is the only way to God the Father and there is no other way except through Him. Be prepared to meet your Maker!

In physical preparation, we need to "understand the times" we live in (1 Chronicles 12:32). This is not achieved by reading secular newspapers and books or watching television or listening to secular radio stations.

Read the Scriptures, listen to Christian radio stations, and get onto the mailing lists of Christian organisations. Read the writings of godly men who "understand the times." If you "understand the times" then you will be prepared to live through it.

You need to be fit. You may be caught in a dangerous situation one day, when even an air force attack would not be able to extricate you from the situation and the best idea would be to run away as fast as possible. You may have to jump over obstacles or gates in your haste to get away; your biggest asset would then be your fitness.

Make good friends; Proverbs 18:24 teaches: "…there is a friend who sticks closer than a brother." You will need friends should you find yourself going through a crisis in your life. I thank the Lord for the wonderful friends He has blessed me with, who stood by me after the massacre. Many telephoned to lend their support, especially after the press criticised my action. Others phoned on the night of the ordeal to find out if I was still alive and well.

Think and pray through the situation. I had thought through what I would do if our church were ever attacked. Ladies need to be prepared to face the possibility of one day being face to face with a rapist, no matter how repugnant the thought. What would you do? How would you react? We need to be continuously on our guard, aware of any eventuality and prepared to act.

Purchase a firearm. Learn to use it properly. If this scares you, buy a tear-gas canister and be ready to spray it into the eyes of your attacker.

Pray. Once you have prepared yourself spiritually and physically for a crisis situation, the most important work of all begins, that of prayer. Prayer does not exempt you from the onslaught of the wicked society in which we live. Nor does being a Christian exempt you from becoming a victim of violence. Pray for wisdom in every situation in which you find yourself. Ask the Lord to help you cope and act in a Biblical way through all of life's hardships.

When I was in a crisis situation like the massacre at St James Church, I realised how important it was for me to know God's Word. It was essential for me to know and understand the Biblical principles of self-defence in both the Old and New Testaments of the Bible. Questions like, "When may I take a life?" or "may I take revenge?" are of paramount importance in this situation. Know the answers to these questions.

You need to decide if you are going to carry a weapon at all and if so, what type? David used a sling, the Apostles had swords and David Livingstone carried a firearm. If you have got this far you need to understand the Biblical principles of when and where to make use of a weapon.

Many times being calm and courteous, while praying imprecatory (war) prayers upon the criminal is the only method open to you. But should the need arise, be wise in the choice and use of your weapon. Other times, give as much resistance as possible and shoot to kill, as this is the only manner possible in which to save innocent lives.

Just remember this—you may have a split second in which to decide what to do! After that, armchair theologians can argue for hours about whether your actions were right or wrong!

After I spoke, I was criticised by one dear brother in Christ, who explained to me that I was Biblically justified in returning fire at the terrorists inside the church while they were attacking innocent people. He then claimed that as soon as the attack had stopped and the terrorists had run outside, my shooting of them there fell into the area of revenge. This was the role given in Scripture by God to the constitutional authorities and not to individuals!

He reasoned that while they were trying to get away, the act of self-defence was over and that revenge in following them on foot and shooting at them was not Biblical. In his thinking and theology this brother was totally correct, if that were the situation.

I explained to him that one of the terrorists was standing next to the getaway car with an automatic rifle, looking at the door from which he expected people to come running out. I am sure he was not waiting to greet them and thank them for coming to the service. So the threat against the lives of the innocent was still there. My actions outside the church were justified!

Furthermore, the South African Police awarded me a certificate of "Commendation by the Regional Commissioner" and it reads:

"Mr Charl Adriaan van Wyk is hereby commended for outstanding services rendered in that he: on 25 July 1993 endangered his own life in warding off the attack perpetrated on the St James Congregation in Kenilworth. His action in pursuing the suspects on foot and returning fire prevented further loss of life. One of the suspects wounded in the incident was later arrested."

Signed: Lt Gen. N.H. Acker 4.10.93.

After the massacre

No respect for God or humankind

SAP 80

Aanprysing deur die Streekkommissaris
Commendation by the Regional Commissioner

MR CHARL ADRIAAN VAN WYK

Word hiermee aangeprys vir besondere
dienste gelewer deurdat hy/sy:
Is hereby commended for outstanding
services rendered in that he/she:

On 25 July 1993 endangered his own life in warding off the attack

perpetrated on the St James Congregation in Kenilworth. His action

in pursuing the suspects on foot and returning fire prevented further

loss of life. One of the suspects wounded in the incident was later

arrested.

LT-C

Streekkommissaris
Regional Commissioner
N H ACKER

WESTERN
Streek ·

G.P.S. (0)

Piles of skulls outside the Ntarama Church, Rwanda, bear testimony to the genocide.

CHAPTER TWELVE

FORGIVENESS

FOR MANY MONTHS after the St James Massacre I struggled with the idea of whether I, according to Biblical principles, had to love the perpetrators of the crime or whether my hatred for them was justifiable. After all, the Bible tells us to love our own personal enemies, but there is no reference to Christians having to love God's enemies.

The other concept I had to deal with was that of "forgiveness." How could I forgive terrorists who had ruthlessly murdered the children of God while they were worshipping Him?

These unresolved questions in my mind played a major role in my decision not to give any interviews to the press or television. I thought that my ideas would conflict with those being told to the media by all others interviewed. Their standard reply to questions was: "We have forgiven the terrorists and we love them, but we hate what they have done!"

My first question was: "How can I forgive somebody if there is no sign of repentance and no request to be forgiven?"

I also did not know whether people could be separated from their acts. Are we not responsible for our sins? Would God let a murderer into heaven one day because He loved the murderer, but hated his sin, supposing he did not repent and come to faith in Christ?

After much reading of the Word and other books and listening to sermons, I believe that I have come to a deeper understanding of these issues from a Biblical perspective.

In his book *War Psalms of the Prince of Peace*, JE Adams deals with one such Psalm, namely Psalm 58, which reads as follows:

> **1.** Do you rulers indeed speak justly? Do you judge uprightly among men? **2.** No, in your heart you devise injustice, your hands mete out violence on the earth. **3.** Even from birth the wicked go astray; from the womb they are wayward and speak lies. **4.** Their venom is like the venom of a snake, like that of a cobra that has stopped its ears, **5.** That will not heed the tune of the charmer, however skilful the enchanter may be. **6** Break the teeth in their mouths, O God; tear out, O Lord, the fangs of the lions! **7.** Let them vanish like water that flows away; when they draw the bow, let their arrows be blunted. **8.** Like a slug melting away as it moves along, like a stillborn child, may they not see the sun. **9.** Before your pots can feel the heat of the thorns—whether they be green or dry—the wicked will be swept away. **10.** The righteous will be glad when they are avenged, when they bathe their feet in the blood of the wicked. **11.** Then men will say, "Surely the righteous still are rewarded; surely there is a God who judges the earth."

The Psalm is not one to be dismissed by an armchair theologian because one would like to use it as a bold war cry against terrorists. Rather, we can make this Psalm our prayer. According to Adams, the lessons of this Psalm are: "First, the accusation of the wicked. Second, the prayer for the destruction of evil. Third, the rejoicing in God's judgement."

Who is doing the accusing in the Psalm?

Only a just man can accuse others of injustice, only someone who is sinless can pray this way. This Psalm is prayed by the innocent man. According to the title, David was the writer of the work, but we know that he was not innocent. How then could he pray it? We know that he was the Lord's anointed in the Old Testament; he was the forerunner of Christ. God was going to bring Christ through David's offspring. David could never have prayed against his enemies this way, in order that his life be preserved. In Psalm 35:12-14 we see that David endured personal abuse. However, Christ was in David, so David's enemies are the enemies of Jesus Christ. So God Himself is accusing the wicked of their guilt through David in this Psalm.

What are the accusations?

(Verse 1) Leaders are silent when the helpless are persecuted and exploited. When you ignore the pleas for help from others, Christ stands up to accuse you of sin. Millions of unborn babies are being put to death around the world while many Christian leaders remain silent. Others justify (at least they try) the murder of the unborn as a "woman's right." They call good what God calls evil and Christ will stand up and accuse them of sin on judgement day. What a frightening thought that is.

(Verse 2) Not only do the rulers of the world fail to oppose injustices, they are also involved in violence and oppression. Before, in South Africa, political parties sanctioned the murder of their opponents in the political arena and certain members of the present government used violent measures to murder "collaborators of the regime." We have exchanged one group of wicked rulers for another.

Since the death penalty has been removed from our country in 1990, over 200,000 innocent people have had the death penalty carried out on them by murderers.

(Verse 3) We are infected with sin even before we are born. This sinful nature results in corruption and causes us to speak lies.

This verse then brings about a change; the tyrants are now being described as opposed to being addressed in the previous verses. We need to recognise that the difference between David and these evildoers is one of degree rather than kind. He was also a sinner from the womb as are all of us.

(Verses 4-5) No one, in and of themselves, will leave Satan's control. You can only be converted by the grace of God. These verses tell of how stubborn and persistent the wicked are in their ways. They refuse to hear God's gracious call to repentance. Neither the greatest preaching nor the most loving persuasion can make them change their minds. They "will not heed the tune of the charmer, however skilful the enchanter may be." If Christ has called us to repentance and we have put our faith in Him while others have not, we cannot become prideful as if it was by our own work. We need to humble ourselves before God and praise and thank Him for making the difference.

Only he who is without sin can hurl these powerful accusations against the wicked.

Can you pray for the destruction of the wicked?

Verses 6-8 contain a straight worded prayer for vengeance on the wicked. We need to be very careful as we look at this.

These prayers were not David's personal vendetta. We know that David prayed for his enemies, and when his prayers went unanswered, he grieved for them as he would grieve for his own mother (Psalm 35:12-14).

While many people have probably tried to use a prayer like this against those who oppose them, that is not what this Psalm is about. We must not pray like this against our personal enemies. We need to show Christ's love and forgiveness to our own enemies and not seek revenge.

Only in Jesus Christ can we pray such frightening prayers for God's justice to be made known on the earth by praying for the destruction of His enemies. From this we learn that God will bring justice upon the wicked. The righteous will be avenged (verse 10). In Deuteronomy 32:35 God says, "It is mine to avenge, I will repay."

God is setting up His kingdom and He will destroy Satan's kingdom as well as Satan's subjects. God alone knows when and how these subjects are going to be destroyed. We need to pray: "Your kingdom come, your will be done on earth as it is in heaven." Christ will do it in His time.

We should pray as the Psalmist did, we have to pray against the enemies of God. Those who will not bow their knees to Jesus should be prayed against, with us asking God to disarm and destroy them. God will bring His judgement upon His enemies and His execution will be fierce. These prayers are going to be fulfilled. God's mighty hand will sweep them away so that all honour and glory will be given to His holy Name.

Can you rejoice when God judges the world?

(Verses 9-11) The only way in which you can rejoice in God's final judgement is if you are in Christ. If you are not, then you will be with those being destroyed.

This Psalm shocks us, but if we reject it, then we are rejecting God and His holiness. We can find deliverance from the judgement of God only in Jesus Christ who bore God's wrath in our place when He died at Calvary. He was afflicted for our wickedness.

The Psalmist's words become Christ's very own. He accuses the wicked and calls down God's judgement upon them. He rejoices with those who are in Him. There will be justice on earth as God delivers the righteous and damns the wicked. This powerful Psalm speaks to each one of us. Where do you stand?

How does this apply to the St James Massacre? I believe that the terrorists are not my personal enemies, they would have attacked the congregation whether I was there or not. They are the enemies of God. What will happen if I pray this prayer against them? Only two things can happen, one is that God's judgement and wrath would fall upon them and they be cast into the lake of fire or that by the grace of God, they come to know Jesus Christ as Lord and Saviour of their lives and then move from being an enemy of God to becoming one of His sons and to me, a new brother in Christ.

I pray that the latter will be the final outcome, but whatever the result, I have to pray against the enemies of God.

I have totally forgiven the attackers for their wrongdoing and bear no malice or bitterness towards them, as is expected of me by God. "For if you forgive men when they sin against you, your heavenly Father will also forgive you. But if you do not forgive men their sins, your Father will not forgive your ones." Matthew 6:14-15

The terrorists, however, do not enjoy the forgiveness of God for their sin, unless they forgive others who have sinned against them. They need to repent from their wickedness and may no longer pursue their old ways.

CHAPTER THIRTEEN

FACE TO FACE

HELLO, I'd like to make an appointment to visit Khaya Christopher Makoma."

"In what capacity would you like to see him? Who are you?"

"I'm the chap that shot him in the St James Church Massacre; I want to come and see him to present the Gospel to him!"

"I'll have to take your number and if he is interested in meeting with you, he can phone you back."

A few weeks later on arriving at my office, the message was on my answering machine. The ex-director of operations of the Azanian People's Liberation Army (APLA), the armed wing of the Pan African Congress (PAC), had left a message! I got in touch with him and he invited me to meet with him at a parliamentary office in Cape Town.

I was about to meet the man who had given the command to attack the church! So much resentment and anger had been dealt with—but still I wondered what sort of man he was. I certainly did not expect to be greeted by Letlappa Mpaglele, with these words:

"Look Charl, this is not an ambush!"

What was this? A terrorist with a sense of humour, a twinkle in his eye? So if it wasn't an ambush—I could relax!

Soon after the initial greetings and pleasantries were exchanged, he was called out to take a telephone call. A young lady from the SABC (South African Broadcasting Corporation), who had heard part of our conversation, popped her head around the corner of the door and asked if they could film our meeting. After some thought, I agreed and so did Letlappa.

I had never given any interviews with regard to the massacre to anybody in South Africa, until that moment. Letlappa and I had to watch what we said on camera as this could be used against either one of us in the future. We sat and chatted for over an hour. I presented the Gospel of Jesus Christ as often as I could, and Letlappa, for his part, tried to justify "fighting for the cause."

On camera, I invited Letlappa to join me in church on the following Sunday, which he unexpectedly agreed to. We made arrangements off camera with the television crew learning all the details.

I kept wondering if I was going to be used by the television crew to advance the cause of the liberal left media. The best I could do was to present the Gospel and pray that the Lord would use the interview for His glory.

Letlappa gave me the telephone number of a friend of his. "This is where I am staying while I am in Cape Town. Please phone me at 7 'o clock on Saturday evening to confirm that all is right for Sunday morning," he asked.

I called and spoke to a woman who said that Letlappa was not there at the time but confirmed that he would meet me at Cape Town Railway Station at 9 'o clock the following morning.

Elton, a friend of mine from Nigeria, accompanied me. When we arrived I noticed that a photographer had also turned up at the station at the same time. He looked around hoping to find us, but when he did not spot us, he drove off. After he had left, Letlappa arrived, exactly on time. I was impressed. His friend, a Mr Gabanka, accompanied him.

We drove off together to St Matthews Church in Table View, which I was attending at the time. I had not told the press that we would be going there. My reason for this was that I sincerely wanted Letlappa to hear the Gospel without any distractions.

The media assumed that we would go to St James in Kenilworth where the massacre had taken place and that was where they waited. I am glad that I did not allow the opportunity to be used by the media—or anybody else for their own gain.

We arrived at the church and sat through the message. Mr Gabanka really enjoyed the service and Letlappa was impressed with the brevity of the message.

After meeting our pastor, Mark Dickson, we promptly left to meet with Khaya in the jail. On the way we had a few good laughs together as we discussed racism and our different cultural backgrounds. I could never have foreseen this kind of interchange between us when I was firing off those shots!

I recognized Khaya as soon as I saw him as we had seen each other during the court case. He is a good-looking, strong, disciplined youth. He and "Happy" (Letlappa's nickname) spoke like old friends, and appeared to be really pleased to see each other.

They spoke in Xhosa, which neither Elton nor I could understand. Letlappa then started telling us what their conversation had been about. He explained to Khaya that he had been to church that morning. Khaya then started laughing, as he thought that his friend attending church was a huge joke! I then spoke up, "I've come to visit you because I want to tell you about the Lord Jesus Christ; you had better keep quiet and listen to me, I didn't come here to waste my time! I have better things to do on a Sunday afternoon than wait in queues here to see you."

Khaya stopped laughing as I started to question him about his position before God. He admitted that he believed that God existed, he even prayed, he said, and believed he was going to heaven because he had been "fighting a just cause!" I had to break the news to him that he was going to burn in hell for what he had done, except if forgiven by our God and Saviour.

He then acknowledged that he was still involved in ancestral worship. I believe that God is a jealous God and you can only come to the Father through Christ, there is no other way for man to approach God except through His Son, Jesus Christ. Synchretism, the worship of various gods, is unacceptable to the Creator of the Universe.

It was time for Letlappa to laugh, he perceived Khaya to have been caught in a trap from which he could not escape. An avowed atheist, he thought himself exempt from the discussion. Mr Gabanka looked at Letlappa and rebuked him, "If you had been listening in church this morning you would not have said that."

I found out that Khaya had had a Bible donated to him and had lent it to a fellow prisoner when he was moved to a different section of the prison. He had not managed to get it back. On my next visit I took another Bible, which had been donated by the Church of Christian Liberty in the USA, along with other Christian literature. It hurt me to see how this young man had been lied to by the liberation theologians in the 1980s. He firmly believed that he would get into Heaven by fighting for a "just cause."

The Bible is very clear about the fact that "good works" or "bad works," for that matter, do not play a part in achieving salvation. Only through putting your faith in Jesus Christ can you be saved by the Grace of God. As you make Him Lord and Saviour of your life, so good works will be the outworking of your faith, not a prerequisite to your faith.

It was only while we were waiting for a bus to collect us from the jail and drop us off outside, that Letlappa found out that I was the person who had shot Khaya on the night of 25 July. He could not believe this. I had assumed that Khaya would have told him, but he had not.

He mentioned that he would never have asked me the question in front of the TV cameras at Parliament had he known. The hypothetical question (as he thought) was: what would I have done if I had been sitting in the exact seat that the man who shot Khaya in the church, had been sitting. Would I have shot back?

He seemed very surprised when I replied: "Yes, most definitely. I believe very strongly in the protection of the innocent."

PART FOUR

CHAPTER FOURTEEN

CRIMINAL RIGHTS

WE ONLY have to open our newspapers to be assailed by the daily horror that man unleashes upon his fellow man. Crime in South Africa is rampant, and most people are becoming inured to the effects of this phenomenon—that is almost considered a normal part of living in South Africa.

Many crimes go unreported—as to do so, would require too much media space. In order to warrant mention in the press these days, a crime has to be so disgusting, so vile, and grotesque, that front-page treatment becomes unavoidable.

One such crime occurred in the quiet, leafy Johannesburg suburb of Roosevelt Park one weekend. On Saturday night, a British woman resident there went into her garden to see why a security light had flashed on. She was immediately grabbed by a knife-wielding young man, who threatened to cut her throat if she tried to raise the alarm.

Dragged back into the house, the terrified woman was bound hand and foot with coat hanger wire, raped twice and forced to commit oral sex. After subjecting her to a six-hour ordeal, her assailant fled with R12,000 worth of jewellery and electronic goods.

The next night, Sunday, three men entered the home of Mrs Burnett-Biddulph, 76 and her disabled husband of 79. They resided in the same Roosevelt Park street. The criminals gained entry into the house by lifting off roof tiles.

The intruders first attacked Mr Biddulph, throwing him from his wheelchair. They then started beating up his wife. Mr Biddulph then crawled to his bedroom where he unlocked his gun safe to access his firearm.

At that moment the rapist of the previous night's attack entered the room and was shot dead by Mr Biddulph. The other two fled and the police arrived.

To the fury of many citizens, the major effort, on the part of the police in this case, was to confiscate Mr Biddulph's firearm for ballistic tests, leaving the couple without protection.

Why should ballistic tests be run on a legally licensed firearm used by the owner in a life-threatening situation? Did they propose charging him with murder? How else was an elderly, disabled man supposed to protect his injured wife against three young, able-bodied thugs? But this confiscation does raise a most critical question in this New South Africa.

A while back, a 65-year-old woman and her husband parked their car in an underground garage in Pretoria. As they stepped from the vehicle, two young men pushed them against the garage wall, demanding money. She cautioned them by saying: "If you injure my husband, I have to warn you that I will shoot you."

As she said this, a third man arrived with a butcher's knife, which he then plunged into her husband's chest.

She shot the attacker in the back of the head with one bullet and killed him. The Sunnyside police confiscated her firearm. In any other civilised country in the world, this would have been treated as a clear-cut case of self-defence, but not here. The police opened a murder docket.

These are not isolated incidents. A police officer on duty shot a hijacker, who was trying to escape. His pistol was confiscated and again a murder docket was opened. The policeman was suspended from duty and later committed suicide because he could not handle his subsequent depression.

So what are the legal rights of firearm owners? Do criminals really enjoy more rights than law-abiding South African citizens? As mentioned elsewhere, the answer to the latter is in the affirmative.

The present government continues to insist on protecting the rights of even the worst offenders, men whose deeds are the echoes of our nightmares. We reiterate that by designing a criminal justice system that denies punitive justice to murderers, rapists and armed robbers, we present the innocent with terror, rape and death at the hands of moral savages—and this on a huge scale. It is also important to consider the endless grief and disarray visited upon those who loved the unfortunate victims. There is no worse pain than to contemplate the suffering of those you love.

Certainly, it is a moral and legal necessity for a civilised society to protect its weakest and most helpless citizens. Capital punishment should be the way that society provides that protection. There are countless cases in South Africa today where the death penalty is the only punishment that could possibly deter such criminals.

The government appears afraid to attempt to address the crime pandemic in any meaningful way. Public anger with the criminal justice system is beginning to boil over, as increasing vigilante actions—in both the cities and townships—are taking place. These people are taking the law into their own hands, and taking it upon themselves to see that a rougher form of justice is done. It is terrifying to contemplate the outcome of such actions.

CHAPTER FIFTEEN

DRACONIAN MEASURES

THE NEW South African Firearm Control Bill (B34D-2000) has now passed both houses of Parliament. It has been approved by the Portfolio Committee on Safety and Security, been voted on by the National Assembly and found its way through the National Council of Provinces.

Once signed by the president, this bill will be called the Firearms Control Act 2000 and will come into effect on a date to be fixed by the president by proclamation in the *Government Gazette*.

In accordance with the bill, applicants would have to pass a competency test and then be issued with a certificate before a licence may be issued. The certificate may only be issued to a person if he or she, amongst other prerequisites:

1. is 21 years or older
2. is a Sout African citizen or permanent South African residence permit holder
3. is a fit or proper person to possess a firearm
4. is of "stable mental condition"
5. has successfully completed the prescribed test on knowledge of the Act.

If there are compelling reasons, the Registrar may allow a person under the age of 21 to apply for a competency test. The certificate lapses after 5 years.

Permanent residency is very expensive and the process may take years due to bureaucratic bungling. The fact that tourists and ex-patriots may want to be armed when visiting "this very safe country," is also not considered.

South Africa has an extremely high rate of illiteracy, and the fact that applicants must complete a written test blatantly discriminates against those people who cannot read or write, but who would still like to be able to protect their families.

The Registrar may also issue a separate licence to every person who resides on the same premises as the holder of the licence in respect of a particular firearm.

Only a shotgun which is not fully automatic, or semi-automatic, or a handgun which is not fully automatic, may be licensed for self-defence. The need for a firearm must be proved to be essential, and only if that need cannot reasonably be satisfied by means other than the possession of a firearm, may a licence be issued.

Who would need a firearm in the new South Africa—we only have the highest murder rate in the world! How does one prove this need, do you first "need" to be attacked before you can prove that you need a firearm?

If we look to other countries where similar laws have been introduced, we will probably find that after a period, the Registrar may decline licences for obscure reasons. Applicants, who in their individual capacity are either unable or unwilling to go to court over their right to own firearms, will rather surrender their arms to the authorities.

This happened in Britain and some people almost bankrupted themselves when they tried to defend their stance in court. Most people will also not support their fellows in fear of their own renewal being rejected later.

Only one licence may be issued for self-defence. No person may hold more than four licences in total for self-defence, occasional hunting and sports shooting. Should he/she have a self-defence licence, this would make available only three licences for sport and hunting.

The Registrar may issue more licences for dedicated hunting and sports shooting separately to the above. The applicant would need to be a registered member of an accredited hunting association or sports shooting organisation. Whatever happened to the freedom of association as set out in South Africa's Bill of Rights?

The only time you may allow another person to use your firearm is while they are under your immediate supervision and where it is safe and lawful to do so.

Application for a new licence needs to be made 90 days before the expiry of an existing licence takes place. Applicants will still need to comply with the terms of the Act and renewal is not automatic.

Licences for firearms used for self-defence need to be renewed every five years and those restricted firearms (semi-automatic rifle or shotgun or any others restricted by the Minister) need to be renewed every two years.

When carrying a firearm it must be completely covered and the person carrying it must be able to exercise effective control over it. At least concealed carry is allowed.

An ammunition limit of 200 cartridges for each licensed firearm is imposed. This does not apply to dedicated hunters or dedicated sports persons.

Besides any fully automatic firearm, the bill specifies any firearm and devices, which are prohibited and may not be possessed or licensed. Over and above this, the Minister may declare any other firearm of a specific type to be a prohibited firearm if it is in the interest of public safety or desirable for the maintenance of law and order.

He may further prohibit or restrict the acquisition, disposal, possession or use of ammunition, or firearm parts in the interest of public safety or if desirable for the maintenance of law and order. What in this Bill would prevent the Minister from declaring all firearms "prohibited?"

A member of a military force of another country visiting South Africa in terms of an international obligation or an agreement between that country and South Africa is exempted from the provisions of the Act, to the extent provided for in the obligation or agreement in question. This clause is indeed a strange one. How is it possible that foreign soldiers should be granted a right that citizens are being denied—in their own country?

A person may be declared unfit to possess a firearm if he/she has failed to take the prescribed steps for the safe keeping of the firearm. Is Big Brother going to peep through our windows to see where our firearms are kept? Or would this involve surprise home searches?

A court may declare a person to be unfit to possess a firearm if convicted of an offence regarding failure to store firearms or ammunition in accordance with the requirements of the Act. Negligent loss or handling of a firearm by the owner or another participant in the offence is also reason to be declared unfit.

Your licence must be carried with you at all times, if carrying your firearm, and it must be produced for a police official if requested. If a person fails to comply, the police official may seize the firearm without a warrant and keep it until the licence is produced. There is also a proposed penalty of a ten-year prison sentence if you forget your licence at home!

Searches and seizures may take place without a warrant by a person authorised by the National Commissioner. Fingerprints, palm prints, footprints and bodily samples may be taken by a police official without a warrant if he suspects an offence punishable for a period of five years or longer. What happened to the right to privacy in our Bill of Rights?

According to this act, a person is guilty until proven innocent. Evidence which raises reasonable doubt will have to be forthcoming to prove innocence in a charge in terms of an offence in which the possession of a firearm or ammunition is an element.

Since the beginning of time, presumption of innocence has been foundational; from the Mosaic Law (Law given to Moses by God) through the Magna Carte (1215), the English Declaration of Rights (1689) and the American Bill of Rights. However, these laws have been replaced by the French Revolution's "guilty until proven innocent" premise. Now it's the case of the State gives, the State takes away.

A person who is aware of the existence of a firearm or ammunition that is not legally owned and fails to report the location to a police official is guilty of an offence and this carries a proposed maximum 15-year imprisonment. How on earth are you going to bring evidence to raise reasonable doubt on such a charge? We will need many prisons for the family members of gangsters. If they tell the police about such an offence, they face the threat of "street justice," but if they remain silent, they face 15 years imprisonment.

If you negligently use a firearm and cause bodily injury to any person, or handle a firearm in a manner likely to injure or endanger any person, you may get 5 years in prison!

An Appeal Board will be established, consisting of no more than five members who must be appointed by the Minister.

Firearm-free zones may be declared by the Minister in consultation with the National Commissioner and Secretary for Safety and Security, if it is "in the public interest" and in accordance with the objects of this act. No firearm or ammunition may be allowed in a firearm-free zone and a police official may search premises and people and seize any firearm or ammunition without a warrant. Suggested imprisonment of 5 years for allowing a firearm in such a zone, 10 years for carrying and 25 years for storage of firearms and ammunition in such a zone are the order of the day!

It is ludicrous to think that criminals are going to leave their firearms at home when entering a firearm-free zone. This merely makes the working environment of criminals safer.

The Minister may, in writing, designate any person or any category of person employed by the State, as police officials.

The St James Massacre in 1993 and the East London pub attack (among many other unreported or unreported upon, incidents) are examples of lives saved by licensed firearm owners returning fire. Several schools in the USA (which are gun-free zones) have been attacked, which proves that the mere status as a gun-free zone does not prevent homicidal attacks. Innocent people had to try to defend themselves with nothing but their bodies.

Fees for licences may be determined by the Minister as well as remuneration to be charged by the dealers for the disposal of firearms.

Thus, the Firearms Control Bill represents a blatantly unconstitutional encroachment upon our rights to privacy, property, life, presumption of innocence and self-defence.

CHAPTER SIXTEEN

HISTORY LESSONS

THE GOVERNMENT wants us to believe that they are the sole protectors and defenders of all South Africans, and that the right to own firearms is the right to arm criminals.

Fallacies such as this are standard rhetoric from the liberal media and non-Christian politicians. It is interesting to note that countries whose leaders have been influenced by Biblical or Christian teaching and who have applied principles gleaned from the Bible into their socio-political structure have seen the right of protection by means of weapons as an inalienable right. It is a God ordained right over which man has no say.

A group of English Protestants of the sixteenth and seventeenth centuries, known as the Puritans, had a decisive role in influencing society. They believed that the Bible was applicable to all areas of life. In 1686, James II of England had ordered the militia to search for and seize muskets and other guns. This proclamation was selectively used against the Protestants—he was Catholic.

Although firearm control laws appear non-discriminatory and are worded to apply universally, they can be used to victimise segments of a population. In June 1688, the leaders of the English Parliament invited William of Orange (the leader of Protestant Netherlands) to come to England and take the throne. William accepted and on his arrival James, having little support, fled to France.

Parliament then enacted the English Bill of Rights (1689). One of the main provisions of the Bill was a guarantee of the right of Protestants to own arms for their personal defence, and not just for the common defence of the nation.

In 1630 many Puritans crossed the Atlantic to the New World. People seeking freedom from oppressive governments formed these settlements. They wanted to establish an ideal state based on Biblical principles. Although they did not establish an ideal society, Puritan morality and theology had a great impact on the culture of future generations.

The issues leading to the American War for Independence should not be trivialised, although it is believed that arms confiscation by General Gage, the British military governor of Massachusetts, played an important role in starting the American War.

Ultimately the American War for Independence resulted in the 1789 United States Constitution being adopted. This was followed in 1791 by its Bill of Rights. The Second Amendment in the Bill of Rights declares: *"A well regulated militia being necessary to the security of a free state, the right of the people to bear arms shall not be infringed."*

When God blessed the children of Israel for their faithfulness, these blessings included a strong national defence and peace. An example of this is during the reign of Jehoshaphat (2 Chronicles 17). The Israelite army was a militia army; each soldier went to war with his own weapon. When Nehemiah rebuilt the walls and gates of Jerusalem, it is noted that even the servants of the Israelites were armed with their own swords.

The Old Testament of the Bible gives a concise historical record of the nation of Israel. It is interesting to note that under the reign of King Saul, the kingdom was lost to the Philistines. The Jews were put into bondage by their victors. The Philistines would not allow the Jews to have blacksmiths in Israel in case the Jews made swords or spears. The Jews had to go to the Philistines to have their ploughshares, axes and sickles sharpened. This all happened as Israel turned away from God and wanted to be ruled by a man rather than God. (Read the account in 1 Samuel 13).

When the Israelites were oppressed by the Philistines during the rule of the Judges, the Bible tells us that they chose new gods and when war broke out there were no spears or swords amongst 40,000 Israelites. The Bible links disarmament with the judgement of God.

Christians were not allowed to own firearms in Turkey. Should a Christian have been found to own a firearm, he would be executed on the spot. This led to the massacre of 1.5 million Christian Armenians in the Ottoman Turkey Empire during 1915-1917. Those who were not killed were enslaved or forced to convert to Islam.

Muslim nations tend not to allow other religious groups in their countries to remain armed. The south Sudanese experience the same phenomenon in Sudan today. The Islamic north imposes firearm control on the south, where the majority of Christians live. The Christians are fighting against the imposition of Islamic (*Sharia*) law.

The Soviet Union in their anti-Christian worldview of Marxism between 1917 and 1953, murdered 36 million peasants and Christians. The Marxist communist agenda has no place for freedom of the individual to bear arms. The Soviet Union used gun registration lists to confiscate weapons in the regions of Georgia, Ukraine and Lithuania. Once again when anti-

Christian governments rise to power, beware of your rights to freedom disappearing.

The Nazis of Germany from 1933 with their ungodly worldview of National Socialism presumed that the government and the people were hostile to each other; so only Nazi party organisations and government officials were exempted from the 1938 gun law's restrictions. The Bible teaches that one law applies to all citizens. The Nazis presumed a government monopoly on ownership of weapons—they assumed this was a privilege granted by the state. Christians teach that weapon ownership is an inalienable right.

On 6 April 1994 a campaign of mass murder was perpetrated against the Tutsi people of Rwanda. The Hutu Animist/Humanist government of Rwanda slaughtered the Christian Tutsi minority groups after enforcing vigorous gun control. Over 500,000 Tutsi Christians were murdered in less than 6 weeks.

CHAPTER SEVENTEEN

FIGHTING BACK

THE POPULACE must not trust governments to be the sole controllers of firearms. Firearms have been blamed for all the genocides (massacres) of Africa; in reality genocides have only taken place in gun-free zones—where attackers have firearms and the defenders do not. When both parties have firearms, we call it a "war."

You need to take a stand on the issue of firearm control; the following projects can help change your country into a criminal free environment:

Organise prayer meetings for the nation, leaders, churches, families, for reformation of the society and revival in the hearts of the population.

Letter writing campaigns: to your government officials, storeowners, magazines and newspapers. Encourage those who are pro-firearms and send letters of protest to those who put firearm owners in a bad light.

Letters to the Editor. This is an excellent way to focus public attention on your issue of concern. You can correct unbalanced reports in your local or national newspapers and magazines.

Speak out publicly. Use every opportunity to speak out about the positive aspects of responsible firearm ownership in your churches, schools and surrounding communities.

Literature distribution. Hand out informational literature to friends and family members to support the responsible use and ownership of firearms.

Stage a peaceful protest. Placard demonstrations in front of government buildings where this issue is being addressed often gets media coverage and always dramatically informs the community of your concerns.

Advertise in the public media. Put up posters in public areas.

Use videos, bumper stickers and T-shirts to get your message across.

Delegations and interviews with influential people. Request interviews with government officials or your local Member of Parliament. Give them a copy of this book and tell them to do something about changing the laws to accommodate firearm ownership. If they do not do what you request, find a leader who will and work the MP out of his seat by campaigning for and supporting a pro-firearm candidate.

Research the enemy and expose them. Find out all you can about gun-free groups and expose their brainless agenda publicly and in the media.

South Africans today have a government that espouses the murder of the defenceless through the legalisation of abortion, a government that shows contempt for women by legalising pornography, and a government that contributes to the destruction of family life through the introduction of gambling and state lotteries.

This same government has not found a solution to the epidemic of crime unleashed on our country. They have introduced the Firearms Control Bill; a Bill that is so immoral as it treats criminals and law-abiding citizens in the same manner. As long as this remains the case, we the law-abiding citizens of the land, will continue to demand the right to protect our families and ourselves.

GLOSSARY

Bakkie: Pick-up vehicle

Frontline Fellowship: Christian organisation that ministers to
        those Christians persecuted in the war zones of Africa

Kop-krapper: Colloquial term for a psychologist

Trommel: Trunk

SWAPO: South West African People's Organisation

UNITA: National Union for the Total Independence of Angola

BIBLIOGRAPHY

Adams JE, *War Psalms of the Prince of Peace: Lessons from the Imprecatory Psalms*, 1991, Presbyterian and Reformed Publishing Company, New Jersey

Aida Parker Newsletter, Issue No. 199, September 1996, Johannesburg

Cain, Miriam, *Make A Difference: A Christian Action Handbook for Southern Africa*, 1999, Africa Christian Action: Cape Town

Stephane Courtois et al, translated by Jonathan Murphy and Mark Kramer, *The Black Book of Communism: Crimes, Terror, Repression* 1999, Harvard University Press, Massachussetts

Firearm News December 2000, Volume IV, Victims Against Crime, Cape Town

Frontline Fellowship News (1993) Edition 4, Frontline Fellowship, Cape Town

Pratt, Larry, *Safeguarding Liberty: The Constitution and Citizen Militias*, 1995, Gun-owners Foundation, Springfield Virginia and Legacy Communications, Franklin Tennessee

APPENDICES

GUN CONTROL
PRECEDES GENOCIDE

Case Studies of Major Twentieth Century Genocide

Perpetrator Government	Date	Targets	Murdered [Estimated]	Date of Gun Control Law	Source Documents
Ottoman Turkey	1915-17	Christian Armenians	1.5 million	1866-1911	Article 166, Penal Code
Soviet Union	1929-53	Christians; Peasants	36 million	1929	Article 182, Penal Code
Nazi Germany & occupied Europe	1933-45	Jews; Gypsies; Christians; Anti-Nazis	13 million	4/12/1928 - 3/18/1938	Law on Firearms & Ammunition; Weapons Law
China	1949-52 1966-76	Christians; Anti-Communists; Pro-Reformers	60 million	1935 - 10/22/1957	Articles 186-7, Penal code; Article 9, Security Law
Uganda	1971-79	Christians; Political Rivals	600,000	1955-1970	Firearms Ordinance; Firearms Act
Cambodia	1975-79	Educated Persons	3 million	1956	Articles 322-8; Penal code
Rwanda	1990-94	Christian Tutsi	500,000	11/21/1964	Law on the Control of Firearms

Total Victims: 114.6 million

OTHER PUBLICATIONS AVAILABLE

By Barlow & Hammond

SA—Renaissance or Reformation?

By Bill Bathman

Angola, By the Back Door
Going Through—Even if the Door is Closed

By Miriam Cain

Fight For Life
Make a Difference

Derek Carlson

Faith & Courage: Commentary on Acts
That You May Believe
Vital Pillars for Missions
Vital Pillars for Reformation

By Eileen Fraser

The Doctor comes to Lui

By Peter Hammond

Biblical Principles for Southern Africa
Biblical Worldview Seminar Manual

Bybelse Beginsels vir Suider Afrika
Die Christen in Oorlog
Christian Action Starter Pack
The Christian at War (also in German)
The Christian Voice of Southern Africa
Discipleship Training Course Manual
Faith Under Fire in Sudan
Finding Freedom from the Pornography Plague
Great Commission Manual
Great Commission Camp Manual 2
Holocaust in Rwanda (also in French)
In the Killing Fields of Mozambique
Muslim Evangelism Workshop Manual
Putting Feet to Your Faith
Security and Survival in Unstable Times

By Christine McCafferty

The Pink Agenda—Sexual Revolution in SA, the Ruin of the Family

By Doc Watson

Fantastic But True: Children's Ministries

Christian Liberty Books

PO Box 358
Howard Place, 7450
South Africa
Tel/Fax: (021) 689-7478
E-mail: clbooks@global.co.za

CONTACT DETAILS

SOUTH AFRICA

Africa Christian Action
PO Box 36129
Glosderry 7702
Cape Town, South Africa
info@christianaction.org.za
www.christianaction.org.za

Firearm News
PO Box 2522
Clarenich 7740
Cape Town, South Africa
firearmnews@frontline.org.za

Frontline Fellowship
PO Box 74
Newlands 7725
Cape Town, South Africa
admin@frontline.org.za
www.frontline.org.za

Gun Owners of South Africa
PO Box 2522
Clarenich 7740
Cape Town, South Africa
admin@gunownerssa.org
www.gunownerssa.org

UNITED STATES OF AMERICA

In Touch Mission International
PO Box 7575
Tempe, AZ 85281 USA
itmi@intouchmission.org
www.intouchmission.org

Gun Owners of America
8001 Forbes Place, Suite 102
Springfield, VA 22151 USA
goamail@gunowners.org
www.gunowners.org

ABOUT THE AUTHOR

Charl is married to Sonja, they have been blessed with four children and they live in Cape Town, South Africa.

Charl is In Touch Mission International's (ITMI) associate missionary to Africa, the Assistant Director of Frontline Fellowship and the Director of Africa Christian Action. He has taken numerous mission trips in southern Africa, organizes and leads evangelistic prayer vigils and is an active conference speaker and radio host.

Charl is contactable for ministry at charlvanwyk@yahoo.com. Financial support for the Van Wyk family is tax deductible in the United States through ITMI. For further information on his work, please contact In Touch Mission International toll-free at 1 (888) 918-4100.

In Touch Mission International
P.O. Box 7575
Tempe, AZ 85281

Phone: (480) 968-4100
Fax: (480) 968-5462
Outside Arizona: (888) 918-4100
General Mailbox: itmi @ intouchmission.org